CHILDREN OF THE EARTH

Other Books by Freddie Langeler

Children of the Stars

Fairies

For information, write to Amber Lotus/Kabouter Products,
1241 21st Street, Oakland, CA 94607. USA

Text: Annemarie Dragt and Dagmar Traub
ISBN 1-56937-101-6
Library of Congress Catalog Number: 95-83109

Printed in Italy

CHILDREN OF THE EARTH

By

Freddie Langeler

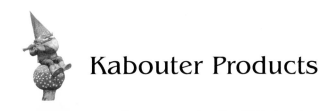

Kabouter Products

Deep down, between the roots of trees,
Live the Earthchildren, who feel at ease.
They are protected in the dark,
While new life is about to spark.

They dream all winter, warm and cozy
Close to each other, their cheeks are rosy.
But now, on earth, it's time for spring:
Rootchildren, Rootchildren, ding-a-ling!

Their mother comes in with a candlelight.
"Dear children wake up, the sun shines bright!
Come see, all these colors I brought for you,
They'll make you look lovely, completely new."

Down by the trees is a good place to dwell:
The roots make nice houses; give shelter as well.
During winter, the children's home is the earth;
Nature gets ready to give a new birth.

The girls are about to leave the ground.
Like little elves they dance around,
Winter is over, now spring comes out,
They will help again to make everything sprout.

You can see how busy they are preparing,
They have new clothes to make, and much repairing.
They embroider, they iron, they cut and they sew;
They work with great care; it's soon ready to show.

"Where are you, mother? Please come and see:
We made pretty new dresses, under the tree.
Pink and red and green and blue—
springbeautiful— you think so, too?"

"Well, let's see," she says, "what you have sewn;
You worked so well, and all on your own.
With dresses colorful and new,
You'll be a fresh and wonderful view."

And look at Ms. Ant, she's eager to know,
What's going on at the cheerful show.
She's looking forward to getting dressed,
Soon she will wear her handsome new vest.

Now look at the boys! Their job is to clean
The creatures on earth, so that they can be seen.
The Root boys scrub and bathe them all,
Ants, beetles, and glowworms, no matter how small.

They paint every being, each one his own style.
As you know there are many, this takes quite a while.
Happily working, they look forward to bring
Once again to the world the spirit of spring.

In the sky vast and blue, the sun shines bright,
Bathing all life in morning light.
You hear the birds? How they rejoice,
Singing a song with cheerful voice.

From their underground home the children climb up,
Each carries a plant: a buttercup,
A snowdrop, grasses, many more—
Bringing life and beauty for us to adore.

A snail inches quietly on his way—
Little Violet shudders, "You go away!
How slimy you are, and you've such big horns!"
Hearing this insult, the snail feels forlorn.

The Earthchildren all make fun of the snail.
"Why have you such a peculiar tail?
You are moving so slow; can you not run?
And what's on your back— is that a big bun?"

"Ho, ho, children, who is shouting so loud?
Is there a reason? Why are you so proud?"
Wise old tree is talking, the children are scared,
To be given a scolding, they were not prepared.

They listen to what the tree has to say;
Ant, fly, and mouse perk their ears up and stay.
"All kinds of creatures live here on earth,
Each one is unique; all are equal in worth."

Reeds and tall grasses are moved by a breeze,
Earthchildren play and feel at ease.
Leaves of the lily serve as a boat,
Two sit in the middle, going afloat.

The water beetle is next for a ride;
Forget-Me-Nots look on from the side.
A dragonfly circling above the lake—
Each being is joyous, each fully awake.

Blossoming flowers swing in the air.
Colors so beautiful, joy everywhere.
Earthchildren and their animal friends
Laugh, hop, and play before summer ends.

Grasshoppers chirp the melody,
Butterflies join the festivity.
The ladybugs celebrate in a ring,
All beings together dance and sing.

Wind rushes the children toward the gate,
Dandelions' seeds fly with featherweight.
Seeds fall to the ground and there take root.
Grow during winter, and in spring become shoots.

Time to come home. Mother welcomes them all,
Ants, bugs, and beetles. It's cold now; it's fall.
The birds fly south. Play comes to an end.
Yet new life is awaiting, like a good friend.